WHATEVER NEXT?!?!
LETTERS TO MY FAMILY ABOUT THE LAST DAYS

LILYANNE JOY

Kingdom Publishers

Whatever Next?!?!

Copyright © Lilyanne Joy

All rights reserved. No part of this book may be reproduced in any form by photocopying or any electronic or mechanical means, including information storage or retrieval systems, without permission in writing from both the copyright owner and the publisher of the book. The right of Lilyanne Joy to be identified as the author of this work has been asserted by her in accordance with the Copyright, Designs and Patents Act 1988 and any subsequent amendments thereto. A catalogue record for this book is available from the British Library.

All Scripture Quotations have been taken from the New International Version and the King James Version of the Bible.

ISBN: 978-1-913247-92-8

1st Edition by Kingdom Publishers
Kingdom Publishers
London, UK.

You can purchase copies of this book from any leading bookstore or email contact@kingdompublishers.co.uk

DEDICATION

First, I dedicate this book to my Precious Lord who has been with me all my life. Without Him, I can do nothing! Then to my treasured sister, DJ, who has encouraged me to take the plunge. Thank you.

My very dear child,

How are you and the family? I have been thinking so much of you all lately and you may be surprised to receive this letter. It is because I think the world of you that I write it.

I have recently seen the film "Left Behind" – have you seen it? It is about this subject that I want to talk to you. Being "Left Behind" is not an idle fantasy – it is an event about which you may not have even heard. The truth is that one day millions of people are going to simply disappear out of this world. The born-again Christians will be taken to be with their Lord. Those "left behind" will face seven or more years of misery, anguish and unmitigated nightmare. Will you be one of the many who will be taken up or will you be left behind? Are you ready my dear? I cannot stress how much I do NOT want you being left behind.

At this point perhaps I should explain "born again". Obviously, we cannot be physically reborn – but we can be spiritually reborn. This is when we ask God to come into our lives, forgive and renew us. What a difference He makes! He loves us beyond words you know. As our Heavenly Father, He loves YOU and wants to share every moment of your life, my dear. Above all, He gives us hope. We cannot live without hope – hope for our todays, tomorrows and beyond into eternity. Of course, you or members of your family may already be born again – that is wonderful! Perhaps someone is a back-slider and turned their back on God. But just in case someone is still outside the Father's family, I feel I must write this letter.

Let me start from the beginning. It is well known that Adam and Eve brought sin on humankind in the Garden of Eden and that separated us from God. Through them we have always lived in a fallen world. Ah – you may not even believe in creation, let alone Adam and Eve. So how do you think it all started? Did everything just arrive? Did all the planets and stars decide what orbits they were going to take? How many other galaxies are there – and did they all just arrive? Perhaps you believe in the Big Bang Theory.

Well, let me explain exactly what happened – "In the beginning GOD CREATED THE HEAVEN AND THE EARTH" *(Genesis 1:1)*. That's it my dear. No ifs, ands or buts. We are then told that "the earth was without form and void" *(Genesis 1:2)* – rather like a lump of clay before the potter does something wonderful with it. "……… and God said let there be…………." Read Genesis chapters 1 and 2 which will tell you how the earth, the heavens, the sun, the moon, the planets and galaxies and all of nature were created. Very beautiful. *Psalm 33:6* says "By the word of the Lord were the heavens made". Did you realise that He named every star! *(Psalm 147:4)*. He created everything ready for when He made humans who were to be His friends.

That's how Adam and Eve come into the story. They were given a perfect and stunning world to live in, nothing was there to spoil their lives. Such a pity they fell into Satan's temptation so soon in the story. They were banished from that beautiful Garden of Eden (to the delight of the devil) and started the human race in pain and sadness. Even their son, Cain, was in-dwelt by Satan because he murdered his own brother in a fit of jealousy. So sad. As time went on humanity was goaded by Satan into being incredibly evil and immoral. *Genesis 6:6* must have one of the saddest sentiments in the Bible – "And the Lord was sorry that He had made man on the earth, and He was grieved in His heart……." God was heartbroken to see mankind, people He created to be His friends and companions, sink to the lowest level of sin, debauchery and idolatry.

That's when He decided to flood the world – keeping only Noah and his family because they were God-fearing, holy people. After the flood, God helped things get back to normal of course, but Satan still insisted on bringing sin to humankind. God promised He would never again flood the world on that scale. He placed a rainbow in the sky as a sign of His promise – His Signature. Remember that next time you see a rainbow, my love.

With that thought, I will leave you because I'm sure you have lots to do. Please think about what I have said.

God bless.

Much love
Auntie Lil

My dearest child,

Oh – I know you are no longer a child but you will always be a dear child to me for I have known and loved you for so long! I have wonderful memories of your childhood capers and times we had together!

If you remember, in my last letter I explained about how God created everything and then created Adam and Eve. It was their disobedience to God that brought the world into sin. Satan certainly thought he had won the day at that time. He even continued to bring evil into the world after the flood.

So, God had to find a way to forgive our inherent wrongdoings (sin) and cleanse us individually. Throughout the Old Testament times it was by animal sacrifice. That was only for God's People, the Jews, though. God decided that the Gentiles (non-Jews) also needed to have a way of forgiveness. You see, we are all sinners and that includes me and you. The Bible tells us that "we have all sinned and come short of the Glory of God" *(Romans 3:24)*. He loved us all SO much and He just couldn't let us be eternally lost. So, He sent His perfect, sinless Son, Jesus, into the world specifically to die to save us all. He designated His precious and only Son to be the ultimate, once and for all sacrifice for us so that we could be forgiven and reconciled to Him. He says in *John 14.6* "I am the way, the truth and the life; no-one comes to the Father except by Me". Jesus died so you don't have to.

I've spoken to you before about the love of God for His children. I don't know whether you have actually taken it in, or taken me seriously. I ask you now to think about these things. We celebrate Christmas as the time when Jesus came to earth as a baby. He grew up to be a carpenter and at 30 years old he went out into the world to do what His Heavenly Father had instructed Him. In the following three years, He showed us what true love was. He patiently healed thousands of people, taught, prayed, enjoyed the company of His disciples – not just the 12 who worked with Him, but all the people who followed Him. I would have loved to have known Him then and been one of the crowds that witnessed His life! Then His life was cruelly cut short by being crucified – but He was crucified for me and you – to give us a chance not to be eternally shut out of Heaven. My dear, I do wish you could just see how much He loves you, wants you to put your trust in Him and be saved.

When Jesus died so agonisingly on the tree, there was a deep darkness over the earth and the veil in the temple was torn from top to bottom. My dear, the veil was 4 inches thick, about 60 feet tall and 30 feet wide and simply could not be torn by human hands. The temple veil divided the public from the Holy of Holies where only priests could talk to God. The significance of this is that when the veil was torn, it was God's invitation to talk to Him direct. Before Jesus died, people could only speak to God through a priest but now we could each have a personal relationship with God. How amazing is that! This is what God wants – a personal and cherished relationship with YOU.

If the death of Jesus had been the end of the story, there would be no hope. But it wasn't. Jesus rose again on the third day just as the prophets had predicted and just as He had told His disciples He would. That means that sin and death have been conquered because He was our final sacrifice. It means, too, that when we receive Him into our lives and hearts, we are forgiven and become children of God. Our physical body is just temporary but we will have a new and perfect body when we go to be with Him. God is King and we become the children of the King to reign with Him forever.

My child, He loves you SO much. Jesus had you in mind when He was dying. He loves you unconditionally. You and members of your family may be very intellectual and think that you are above this 'religion'. It is not religion – it is a relationship. When Jesus was on earth, even he didn't like or trust the religious people. Faith, on the other hand, is something between you and God. I'm not religious as you know, but I have a wonderful relationship with Jesus and that is what my faith is all about. With God there are no boundaries or conditions – He loves us whether we are rich or poor, whatever colour, creed or culture we are, whether we are good, bad or indifferent. Everything is in the Bible – read it my dear, read it.

Well, that's it for now. I will leave you to mull over how much Jesus loves you and wants a relationship with you.

God bless you and yours,

Much love
Auntie Lil

Well, my dear child,

I'm back with just a little more of what's next………. I hope you have considered the joy you can have by asking Jesus into your life.

I tell you this - when you have God in your heart, you have a Friend for life – one who will stick closer than a brother wherever you are in the world. He has promised "I will never leave you nor forsake you" *(Hebrews 13: 5)*. God cannot lie *(Titus 1:2)*, He cannot renege on His promises, He cannot just let you go to the dogs. He loves you with a passion, He cares about you, He takes an intimate interest in you and all you do, because you are His child. Did you know that he numbers every hair of your head *(Matthew 10:30)*? And that He stores all your tears in a jar *(Psalm 56:8)* because He loves you so much. The Bible tells us He is interested in every little detail of your life. He cares.

He said "Behold I stand at the door and knock. If anyone hears my voice, I will come in to him ……." *(Rev.3:20)*. He is just waiting for you to invite Him in. There is a God-shaped hole in your heart, in your life – nothing and no-one else can fill that hole.

Remember, you have the choice whether to accept Him or reject Him. He has promised us eternal life in the most beautiful place – no more pain, suffering, tears, illness, death, hunger, wars, separation, poverty. Imagine what a glorious place we will have in Heaven. The Bible gives us glimpses of Heaven's glory all the time.

Of course, you and your family or friends may say you don't believe in the Bible. You believe in history, don't you? The Bible is proven to be historically correct. All the prophecies in the Bible have been fulfilled to this moment in time. It goes further than that though. You can find something of everything in the Bible and although these things were recorded over many thousands of years, the Bible remains entirely up-to-date. It has much to say to us if we would only listen. There is so much comfort, peace and wisdom that can be had from the Bible. It is God's letter to humankind. Try reading it – you will find it speaks to you.

The Bible is totally relevant to today's world. Did you realise that it foretold aeroplanes, world-wide media etc.? Obviously, they had to use euphemisms as they didn't know the names of such things – "fly like doves" for instance!! The Bible says that the "whole world" will hear the Gospel of Jesus Christ. We have that facility now with all the electronic means of communication – television, YouTube, social media, internet and more. In the last 30 years things like this have leapt forward in a way that our grandparents would and could never have imagined. I certainly can't keep up with it that's for sure!

Although this is only a short letter, I'm going to close now but ask that you think about what I have said. I'll write again before long. Give the family a hug for me!

God bless and keep you.

My love
Auntie Lil

Dearest child,

I hope this letter finds you well. I'm sorry it's been some time since I wrote.

Have you thought about what I said in the last letter? Have you started to read the Bible – God's letter to his beloved children? Well, I promised I would write again and here I am to explain a few more things.

The reason that Adam and Eve were tempted into sin was, as you know, because of Satan. He has other names, the devil, the serpent, the evil one. You may not believe in Satan but he is as real as you or me. Originally, he was a glorious angel named Lucifer but he wanted to be bigger, greater and more powerful than God. He rebelled against God and took a third of the angels away into his rebel camp. From there they have been plotting the downfall of humanity ever since. As a result, there has always been the battle between good and evil – and believe me, Satan and his minions are evil. Satan may win a few battles because people can be pawns in his hand. However, God is victorious in the end.

God doesn't make bad things happen as is often suggested. We live in a fallen world and when Satan has the upper hand it is because he has played mankind at their own game of self-will. God has given us the gift of free will and, being a gentleman, never imposes His Will on us. He will not take away that free will. We can choose how we will live our lives, the decisions we make, the paths we will take – and Satan has a great time helping people make wrong and cruel decisions! However, God does mitigate the outcome. Take 9/11: according to the statistical information, there should have been 50,000 people working in those twin towers (with some 140,000 visitors) most of whom could have been killed. Instead, God made people late, traffic jams, delayed trains etc. then held the buildings up long enough for most people to escape. Just under 2,900 died - 2,900 too many but the devil was rubbing his hands in glee nevertheless. (A further 234 died in the other two air strikes – it could have been so many more). All these figures can be found on the internet my dear – check them out.

NEVER underestimate the power of Satan – and NEVER underestimate the love of God for His children. God gives you the power to conquer Satan.

Mankind, at the instigation of Satan, has decided to remove God from schools, colleges, boardrooms, life and even churches. Don't you see - without God, we are in a pickle. He created the world; he designed and created the universe in which our earth hangs. He invented physics, astrophysics, geophysics, mathematics, languages – He designed and created every single thing in the universe – including YOU and ME. We are so wonderfully and intricately made. He knew you and loved you even before you were born. It tells us this in the Bible. That's why you are so very precious to Him and He does not want to lose you. Why don't you read *Psalm 139* for a glimpse into God's heart of love and care for you?

As you know, things in the world are getting increasingly difficult; evil abounds, immorality has now become the norm. There is financial upheaval, terrorism, nuclear threats, deadly diseases for both nature and humans. Then there are the earthquakes, volcanoes, tsunamis, flooding, cyclones, drought, famine and other natural disasters increasing. If the Bible had not already foretold all these things, we could be wondering what on earth is happening. But the Bible has told us these things are going to happen – and happen more and with greater impact on our lives. Thank goodness God has given us the opportunity of peace, serenity and safety in His love for us – as long as we have given our lives into His safekeeping. He wants our names to be written in the Lamb's Book of Life so that our future is secure in Him. Jesus died for us; He loves us that much. "For God so loved the world that He gave His only begotten Son that whosoever believes on Him should not perish but have everlasting life" *(John 3:16)*.

At this point I want to remind you that whilst God had a Son, Jesus, He is a triune God. God the Father, God the Son and God the Holy Spirit. You know about God, you know about Jesus, but you may not know the purpose of the Holy Spirit. Jesus told us that when He went back to His Father in Heaven after His resurrection, the Comforter would come and dwell in us (read *John 16; 7, 8)*. The Comforter is the Holy Spirit. The Holy Spirit lives inside each person who has put their life in God's Hands. He guides, He comforts, He strengthens, He is all in all to those who love God. He is God inside our hearts, we are His residence on earth so we are never alone.

That brings me to the subject of my first letter about being "Left Behind". The Bible tells us – and indeed, Jesus told us – that one day "in the twinkling of an eye" *(1 Corinthians 15:52)*, all truly committed and born again Christians will disappear. We will have been taken up into Heaven to be with the Lord – out of this troubled world. The Holy Spirit will also leave the earth because He inhabits the hearts of born-again Christians. You must understand my dear, the Holy Spirit through God's people, has been restraining the devil's work. The Bible tells us "....... I will send Him (the Comforter) to you, and when he has come, he will reprove (i.e., rebuke, censure, condemn) the world of sin......" *(John 16:7,8)* This means he has kept Satan's scheming at bay, kept God's children from the worst of Satan's machinations. *2 Thessalonians 2:7,8* also tells us that when the Holy Spirit has been taken out of the way, then Satan is free to do what he wants, through whom he wants, how he wants.

So, once we and the Holy Spirit have left the earth, imagine the brutality that will follow now that Satan has a completely free hand. (I'll tell you about that in another letter perhaps). God has given us an "escape" by inviting us to trust in Him – now *(Luke 21:36)*. Time is short.

Without being a sensationalist, let's look at the result of the "Rapture" which is what Christians have named this calling away. (It comes from the Latin word rapere which the Greeks translated as harpazo which means "snatched away"). The Bible tells us that two will be in bed and one will disappear: two will be working side-by-side and one will go – you get the idea. Across the world there will be chaos – banks and shops, restaurants, hospitals, schools, colleges, universities, waterworks and power stations depleted of staff, governments weakened – the list goes on. Just imagine it my love. That's part of why I want **you** to be among the Raptured ones – I really don't want you or any of your beloved family to be left behind and nor does God. If I, a mere human, can love you with such depths of love, how much more will God love you, the person He created, the person Jesus died for. You are so precious.

I pray for you and each member of your family constantly that you will make the choice to follow Jesus, to ask Him into your life. You have nothing to lose and everything to gain by just saying "Please Jesus, come into my heart". Think about it. I ask again – are you ready? If you died today, would you be ready for eternity.

God bless you as you contemplate what I have said – but please don't leave it too long.

Love as always,
Auntie Lil

My dearest child,

I do hope you are all keeping well. As promised, here I am, back again to continue the story – His Story.

As I said in my last letter, millions of people across the world are going to disappear one day – just as in the film. The ones left behind will then really begin to feel their absence. Banks won't open, shops will have a severe shortage of staff and the shelves will not get filled because deliveries will be curtailed. Indeed, food supplies in general will become difficult to obtain. Hospitals, doctors' surgeries, care homes, schools, universities, postal services, air traffic control etc. will not function. Chemists will be unable to supply medication if the pharmacist has been taken. Farms will not be able to supply milk, eggs, grain or meat if their staff are depleted. Governments will be in disarray because so many of their number will have gone – even, perhaps, Prime Ministers or Presidents – yes, even they can be born-again!! We've seen a hint of this chaos caused by the Coronavirus and that's been bad enough!!

It will be surprising the people who have disappeared – and equally, the people who have been left behind. Yes, there will be vicars and church ministers who led a 'religious' life but were not born again. As in Jesus' day, the religious leaders were very pious and 'served' God in the temple, but they often did not have a heart for God. It was they who were instrumental in sending Jesus to the cross.

After the rapture Russia and its Muslim allies (viz. all the "Stans", Turkey, Egypt, Iran, Ethiopia, Libya and more) will take advantage of the total world chaos to gather an army together to attack Israel. They will see that everyone's attention is elsewhere and this is a splendid time to sneak in and eradicate Israel. But remember what I said in the past, that the One who guards Israel neither slumbers nor sleeps – and God sees exactly what they are up to! They themselves will be eradicated in an amazing series of events which includes an earthquake, possibly a volcano – indeed, who knows what God will pour down on them for attempting to hurt HIS PEOPLE. In the book of Revelation, it has a detailed description of what will befall these armies.

The entire world will be in chaos, make no mistake about it. However, eventually out of the mess a certain person will come to the fore to take charge of everything. He is called "The Antichrist". Daniel tells us that he will have great intellect, will look impressive but will be very cunning and deceitful. He will make decrees that will quite quickly make order out of the chaos (because he is Satan's emissary and has his help). He will have an associate who will be a religious leader – he is called "The False Prophet". To begin with Governments and the general public will think these two people are wonderful. They will be considered 'sensible', 'remarkable' and 'all powerful'. How do I know all this? It is prophesied in the Bible and until now every Biblical prophesy has taken place so I don't doubt its validity now.

I remind you what I said in my last letter – the Holy Spirit who has always been restraining Satan's schemes, has been taken out of the world at the Rapture. So now Satan has the world to himself, unfettered, totally unimpeded and unrestrained. He can do exactly as he likes and he can make humanity do his bidding. I have to admit that most people left behind will be pleased the "Bible-preaching" people have gone, because now, they won't have them pricking their consciences!

These two individuals, the Antichrist and the False Prophet, will use the chaos, confusion and total lack of leadership to become the leaders of the world. Know that Satan is the Boss-Man of the Antichrist and False Prophet and he has enormous powers he can bestow on these two evil beings. The Antichrist will be welcomed as a miracle-worker and soon take control of world governments.

A World State and economy will be introduced. Some will resist but most will be glad to have someone who will lead them. One world religion will be instigated and woe betide anyone who does not obey.

I am serious, my treasure, when I say please consider your spiritual welfare. Ask Jesus into your heart so that you know, without a shadow of doubt, that you are safe.

God bless – and loads of love,

Auntie Lil

My dear cherished child,

How are you and the family? Hopefully you are all well and keeping busy – not too busy to seriously consider what I am trying to convey to you through my letters. Of course, I shall see you sometime soon and we can discuss things further, but for the moment, I must continue to show you what lies ahead.

I think I told you in my last letter about the Antichrist and False Prophet. These two people are real, real people, my child. Do not be under any illusion. Do not think that they are some fairy story characters. Take them seriously. And another thing – HELL is a real place, too.

When they take command of world affairs, and in his new position as leader of the world, the Antichrist will make a treaty with Israel guaranteeing their safety. That heralds a period of seven years, called The Tribulation. Israel will be allowed to build a new Temple. (You know, they have all the plans, the materials, the sacred artifacts for use in the Temple already in place for that promised day!!) However, in the middle of the seven-year period, the Antichrist will show his true colours and break his treaty with Israel – he never intended to keep it anyway! This three and a half year period is called The Great Tribulation. This is because not only will The Antichrist and False Prophet wield enormous power and make life well-nigh impossible, but natural catastrophes will multiply on an unprecedented scale. All sorts of things happening which are all part of Bible prophesy. Be safe my dear, dear child – claim God as your Saviour before it's too late. You don't have to go through all this.

At the same time, these two will begin to insist that everyone throughout the world have a mark on either the back of the hand or on the forehead. When once they have had everyone marked, they demand that everyone bows down and worships the effigy of the Antichrist – a one-world religion. This huge, animated effigy of the Antichrist will be situated in Jerusalem. Anyone not worshipping the Antichrist <u>will be executed</u>. One of the Ten Commandments is "You shall have no other gods before me………. **<u>You shall not bow down to them or worship them</u>**" *(Exodus 20:3-5)* (my emphasis).

HOWEVER……………. the other side of the coin is this. Whilst everyone who takes the mark of the Antichrist will be able to conduct a reasonable lifestyle here on earth, they will <u>never</u>, <u>ever</u> be able to enter God's eternal life. This is just what Satan wants, of course. He is determined to see as many people go to hell with him as he possibly can. Satan lies. Satan hates humanity and he hates God. He will use Scripture and falsehoods, miracles and wonders to persuade you that HE is the true god and that our God is a myth. Ignore that. Trust God and know that God is real. God is ultimately in control – trust Him please.

Now it seems that people are between a rock and a hard place. To bow or not to bow; to receive the mark or not to receive the mark. But that is not the case really. You can escape this scenario *(Luke 21:36)* by genuinely giving your life to the Lord NOW – before all this happens. As I said before, God has provided salvation for everyone who will claim it. He wants no-one to go through the seven years of hell on earth that will be Satan's paradise, and still miss out on eternal life at the end of it. You see, if you have already given your heart to God, you won't have to make this decision. You'll be in a better place already.

DO remember, though, that God can see the heart and He knows whether your decision is real or not. Believe me dear, a life with God in it is so much better, deeper, fuller. richer than without Him. You will find immeasurable peace and inner joy whatever befalls you in life or death. How can you not invite Him into your heart? As He declares in *Jeremiah 29:11* "I know the plans I have for you, plans to prosper you and not to harm you, plans to give you hope and a future." What a promise! Whether He comes again tomorrow or in ten years' time; whether you die before He comes, life with God in it is so much better. He gives us Victory – Victory over Satan, over sin, over death. You need never be afraid of dying because you will know that you are entering God's wonderful presence. He has such a welcome party waiting for you.

Jesus said "Let not your heart be troubled neither let it be afraid" *(John 14: 27)*. In these uncertain days, we need to rest on that promise. We simply have to have someone to trust in, someone who will protect, guard and guide us. Don't let silly pride stop you from making a decision for Jesus and His eternal life promise. I urge you to read the Bible – start by reading the Psalms and the four Gospels of the New Testament, particularly what Jesus has to say in *Matthew 24*. They will give you great insight and comfort.

I'll leave you with these thoughts. Please think long and hard about what I have told you, my dear. Don't put your eternal life in jeopardy. Ask Jesus into your heart now and be ready.

God bless, love as ever,

Auntie Lil

Well, my dear child,

I hope you are all well. I am sorry my last letter was rather long but have you thought about what I have told you? Have you made a decision that will keep you safe with God? I do hope so. He loves you so very much and died to save you. "No greater love has any man than that he lays down his life for his friend" *(John 15:13)* – and you are His Friend.

Now, I was telling you in my last letter that Satan will have the world to himself for the next seven years and will rule cruelly through his two agents. The Christians will have left the earth – but there is hope even now. You see, there will be people who know that they should have given their lives to Jesus but never did, who will make that decision now. There will be people who suddenly realise that they are left behind, that this is for real - and they, too, will make their decision. (***You*** may even have to make that decision). Life will be much more difficult because they cannot accept the mark of the beast, and they may well get executed. BUT................and this is the thing - **they will be welcomed into Heaven, into the arms of Jesus** and all will be well with them. Many will hide and live on the land, or be provided for by kind people who perhaps have taken the mark (who knows?). God has provided a safe place for His People and in *Matthew 24:16* He told them to flee to the mountains for their safety

In the first half of the Tribulation, there will be two remarkable Witnesses assigned by God who will continue to proclaim the Saving Grace of Jesus and they will bring many people into the Kingdom of God. The story of these two mighty men is amazing – I'll tell you about them another time perhaps. These two Witnesses will be called back into Heaven in a spectacular way (Read *Rev.11*). However, there will be other messengers and witnesses to take their place that will come from the Jewish people to spread the gospel to the whole world. God is so anxious that everyone throughout the world has the chance to be saved.

I just don't want any of you to be left behind in the first place. I am not being an alarmist, to frighten you into making a decision for Jesus. That is your decision entirely. I am just telling it as it is – read all about it in the Bible. As born-again Christians we have such a hope and expectation of eternal life that things on earth should not frighten us since we are God's children. Of course, we wouldn't be human if we did not feel some concern!

There are many, many prophecies in the Bible about these end times – both in the Old and the New Testaments. Even Jesus talked about them. One of the things He said was "When you see these things begin to happen, look up............." *(Luke 21:28)*. We are seeing these things begin to happen and so we should be prepared and make sure we are ready. Join me in "Looking up"!!!!!!!

Please think about these things my dear. You are precious to me and your life and spiritual welfare weighs heavily on my heart. You are constantly in my prayers.

Lots of love as always,

Auntie Lil

Dear child of mine!!

How are you all? Do hope you are all well. Once again, I ask, have you thought about the subject of my last letter? Indeed – have you thought about the contents of ALL my letters? Well, now we are getting to the more intense period of time so I will continue.

As I told you in a previous letter, Satan's prime objective is to eliminate Israel – indeed, this has always been his fundamental purpose ever since God designated Israel as His people. All down through the centuries there has always been some fanatic trying to eradicate the Jews. There are far too many radical groups for me to list but here are just a few: the Abyssinians; then in Esther's time there was Haman who plotted to kill all the Jews (that's a story you really should read, my dear). There were the Babylonians, Crusaders, Egyptians, Romans, and in latter years, the Nazis. Nowadays it is the Islamists. But God has always protected His people. That's why there is still a Jewish nation even though so many of them were killed and others scattered throughout the world.

This now becomes the Antichrist's mission – to eradicate Israel and the Jews, having already (he thinks) wiped out the 'Jesus' people with his executions. I don't know where he thinks the 'raptured' people have gone! We are in Heaven with our Lord waiting for the next event. I have to remind you that Satan, through the Antichrist, also wants to remove God from existence. God is Satan's archenemy and he will do anything to exterminate both God and the Jews.

The land of Israel belongs to the Jews because God gave them that land – and He will not allow anyone to take it from them again. Did you know that the Bible prophets said that Israel would become a State again – and Britain was instrumental in that in 1917 with the Balfour Declaration. In 1948 Israel became a State in its own right. God also says that He will gather His People, the Jews, back to Israel from all around the world where they have scattered to take refuge – and that's happening now. Millions of Jews are "coming home" to Israel. Incidentally, God promised Israel "I will bless them that bless you and I will curse them that curse you" *(Genesis 12:3)* – remember that.

So, it is because of Satan's anger and hatred of God and the Jews that even now he is stirring up the Middle Eastern countries to 'bomb Israel out of existence'. The situation out there is tenuous to say the least. God will protect Israel. He has said so. He certainly has in the recent past. However, there will come a time when many countries will band together under the Antichrist's banner with their "prime directive" to annihilate Israel.

At the risk of repeating what I said in a previous letter, I have to remind you that the Antichrist will be thoroughly evil after he breaks his 'peace agreement' with Israel because now he no longer needs to pretend to be the 'wonder-working' benign leader. I can't begin to tell you what things he will do. One thing is certain, his insistence on EVERYONE receiving his mark will take top priority. Anyone not taking the mark will be banned from any financial transaction as I told you. Anyone who has invited Jesus into their life since the Rapture will not and cannot take the mark so life will be well-nigh impossible and very likely forfeit. Remember, those taken up at the Rapture will be safe with Jesus.

At the end of seven years, the Antichrist and False Prophet will gather armies from around the world to wage war on Israel. It will be the worse war ever experienced but God will annihilate the aggressors – the Bible tells us so. God will claim the Victory with trumpets and hallelujahs and all His Saints (that's those who were caught up at the Rapture) will be with Him at this, His Second Coming – **and every eye shall see Him** *(Rev.1:7) (my emphasis)*. The Book of Revelation explains the whole scenario and it makes amazing reading. That will be the end of our world as we know it. God will create a New Heaven and a New Earth. We who are His children, will enjoy such beauty, peace and glory – even I find it difficult to comprehend what being with Jesus will be like in the New Heaven and New Earth. Everything will be more vibrant, colourful, beautiful that ever before. Even the animals will be gentle. Oh, my dears, I do hope you are there to share it with me!

Think about what I have told you. Invite Jesus into your heart, into your life and claim His salvation. You know it makes sense my dear one.

God bless you and the family,

Much love
Auntie Lil

Dear Precious Child,

I think this will have to be the last letter on this subject. It is such a vast topic and I don't want you to be overwhelmed with information. That is why I have given small chunks in my letters! You know me – I could letter-write for the Olympics!!!

Have you thought about my previous letter? Have you and your loved ones discussed the implications of what I have told you? I do hope so. We can talk about things when I am next with you. In the meantime, go to a good solid evangelical church near to where you live, talk to the minister there and he will help you get to know our wonderful Lord.

Now, to continue from my last letter. After the war has ended with God victoriously supreme, what happens to Satan and his two henchmen? Well, the Antichrist and the False Prophet will be thrown into the fires of hell to live there for eternity. Satan, too, will be bound in the bottomless pit but only for a thousand years. When these evil-doers have been dealt with, there will be 'peace on earth and goodwill towards men' because God will reign supreme in the New Heaven and the New Earth for one thousand years. Our world will be so beautiful and kindness and gentleness will prevail. Truth, love and peace will become normal and there will be nothing to spoil our day. Above all, we will live in the light of God, the love of Jesus and the freedom of the Holy Spirit. That's something to look forward to, isn't it?

At the end of the thousand years, Satan is released for a short period of time to see if there are any people on earth that he can lead astray who are not fully committed to the Lord. You see, in that thousand years, children will be born who will have children. Those children may not follow in their parents' and grandparents' love for the Lord; hence Satan may have a little harvest. There cannot be any sin in the Heavenly Kingdom. After that God will deal with Satan as He sees fit. You have to remember that he was once an angel and cannot be dealt with in the same way as the other two who are purely human.

Also remember that the Bible tells us that "**every** knee shall bow ......and **every** tongue confess......" *(Romans 14:11) (my emphasis)*. That means everyone, whatever their beliefs in their human lifetime, WILL acknowledge God. Unless they have acknowledged Him in this earthly life, no-one will have the right to eternal life with Him in Glory. Be aware that everybody will be judged before God – but if you have your name in the Lamb's Book of Life, Jesus' blood spilt on Calvary has redeemed you. We will be judged differently with this in mind – unlike those who have made the decision to have nothing to do with God. *Psalm 53:1* says this "The fool hath said in his heart 'There is no God'.........." Please don't be classed as a "fool", my dear one.

I have only given you a brief outline, a snapshot of things to come, my dear. It is all very much deeper, intense and more complex than I can explain in a letter. When I next see you, we will perhaps have time to talk about things in more detail. You are bound to have questions. In the meantime, read the Bible, make your decision for Christ, begin your journey with Him – He will carry you through all things and give you peace beyond understanding. And you will escape the dire consequences of the seven years Tribulation.

Find a good evangelical church to attend in order to worship with like-minded people.

God bless you my dearest child.

Much love
Auntie Lil

PS:

My Dear Loved Ones,

It was great to see you and have long chats even though it was quite some time ago. I hope I answered your many questions adequately! There are so many things we don't understand about the end times, but what we **do** know we must take seriously.

Since being with you many things have happened throughout the world which I must bring to your attention. To begin with, earthquakes and volcanic eruptions have been on the rise according to volcanologists and seismologists. Famines, lack of rain, too much rain, larger and more frequent tornados and storms, plagues such as the locusts in Africa, humongous fires, to name but a few of the things happening. Did you know there are about 1,500 viably active volcanoes around the world and a myriad more on the seabed! According to meteorologists wild weather is also on the increase — and mankind cannot stop or alter this in spite of protestors! If you want to check my statements, go on the internet and you will see for yourself.

The Bible says that these things will occur more frequently in the end times. Jesus said "When these things begin to happen, look up for your salvation is near" *(Luke 21:28)* – that's the Rapture. Our world is becoming a very evil and topsy turvy place but God has plans for a peaceful and lovely earth, as I've told you in one of my letters. Time is short. I suggest you read books by David Jeremiah, Amir Tsarfati, and John Hagee to begin with, or even watch them on YouTube.

Recently the world has experienced the Coronavirus as you know. The question has arisen, of course, whether this is one of the prophetic plagues of the end times. I believe this is just a taster, a precursor, a sample of what is waiting in the wings after the Rapture - only then it will be much, much worse. It was amazing how quickly it mushroomed and was a salutary example of just how rapidly a disease can spread around the globe. The world is a small place nowadays with travel so easy and so delightful! Many of us go to places our forebears would only have imagined in their wildest dreams. The brave ones travelled, of course, but it could have taken weeks or months to get to their destination. Now, we could visit six countries in the time it took them to get to one!! Imagine – on a cruise people can visit 6-8 countries in two weeks! A 'plane can take us to the other side of the world in 24 hours. What would the people of the Bible say about that!

My treasured ones, please, please take these things seriously and make a decision to follow the Lord. I cannot lose you; you are too precious. Please don't be left behind because things are going to get 100 times worse than we have had it up until now as I am sure I explained in my letters. May God become your Rock, your Salvation, your everything. He gives everlasting life, forgiveness, peace and so much love. Remember, Jesus died because of His deep, unconditional love for you. We're at the 'finish line' – please ask Him into your heart now.

You are in my prayers constantly. May God bless and keep you.

Lots of love,
Auntie Lil

www.ingramcontent.com/pod-product-compliance
Lightning Source LLC
Chambersburg PA
CBHW021200080526
44588CB00008B/437